Why Do You Think I Call You Mama?

A Journey Through Dementia

Why Do You Think I Call You Mama?

A Journey Through Dementia

Deborah Keys

REDEMPTION
PRESS

Published by Redemption Press, PO Box 427, Enumclaw, WA 98022 Toll Free (844) 2REDEEM (273-3336).

Redemption Press is honored to present this title in partnership with the author. The views expressed or implied in this work are those of the author. Redemption Press provides our imprint seal representing design excellence, creative content and high quality production.

Unless otherwise indicated, all Scripture quotations are from The Holy Bible, *English Standard Version*® (esv®) Copyright © 2001 by Crossway, a publishing ministry of Good News Publishers. All rights reserved. esv Text Edition: 2007.

ISBN 13: 978-1-63232-895-3 (SC)
⠀⠀⠀⠀⠀⠀⠀978-1-63232-899-1 (HC)
⠀⠀⠀⠀⠀⠀⠀978-1-63232-900-4 (ePub)
⠀⠀⠀⠀⠀⠀⠀978-1-63232-905-9 (Mobi)
Library of Congress Catalog Card Number: 2015960016

This book is dedicated to my mom and dad who taught me how to be a caregiver by example.

Acknowledgments

*V*ery special thanks to:

God, first and foremost, for giving Mom and me grace each and every single day.

My family who were willing to Mom- and Grandma-sit, so I could have much-needed, short respites along my journey.

My many precious friends who adopted Mother Keys as one of their own. They were always thoughtful to ask about her and patiently listened to all of my Mama stories. When she was able, Mama would join us for a casual dinner out, or at home when we would enjoy potluck.

Dr. Walter Beebe who for many years expertly and compassionately cared for Mom's vision.

Dr. Jayaprakash Reddy and Dr. Marina Vengalil who kept Mom as healthy as she could be for many years.

Carla, Mom's hairdresser/stylist. Mom was even more beautiful after a visit to your salon.

A Place for Mom, especially Tracey Fitzgerald, for support while finding a place for my mom and sponsoring the "Rest and Recharge" contest.

Joan Lunden, former host of *Good Morning America* and current national spokesperson for A Place for Mom, for awarding me the "Rest and Recharge Caregiver Vacation" I enjoyed at Camp Reveille. What a wonderful final chapter of Mom's stay with me, and a refreshing start to beginning my new life.

The nurses, CNAs, doctors, and staff in the Abri Memory Care Unit for your service and patience.

My sweet friends Kelsey, Noma, Jan, Lucia, and Kris who helped me proofread and edit these words you are reading. You listened, sympathized, laughed with me, and cried with me.

You . . . because you chose to read this very personal journey of my mom and me.

Why Do You Think I Call You Mama?

"Where did you go to school?"

What an odd question, I thought. She should know the answer to that! After all, she and Dad helped pay for college. Okay. I'll play. "Eastfield for the first two years, then on to Stephen F."

"Debbie did, too."

I looked at Mom. "Who is Debbie?"

"My daughter," Mom answered.

"Who am I?" I asked quizzically and with furrowed brow.

"Aren't you my niece or my relative?"

That Sunday afternoon conversation, sitting on a bench on the front porch, was the moment in time I realized my own mother did not know who I was. My heart shattered into a billion pieces.

Exodus 20:12 states, "Honor your father and your mother, that your days may be long in the land that the LORD your God is giving you." Even if it was not a commandment with a promise, I would still abide by and obey this verse. It was my honor and privilege to be the sole caregiver in my home for my sweet and devout Christian mother for more than five years. Gathering around the kitchen table for family meals, and saying grace before we ate was the norm. Mom and I continued to give thanks to God at mealtime, even after she moved in with me. If she became confused or forgetful while praying, she always said God knew what she meant. I believe He did.

After falling and breaking her hip, having hip-replacement surgery, going through rehab, falling and breaking her hip again, having a second hip-replacement surgery and going through rehab again, in June 2008, my mom moved in with me for in-home rehab and memory care.

As her condition deteriorated, my caregiving duties increased and became more involved. Though everything I did came from a heart of unconditional love, it wasn't easy by any stretch of the imagination. Every single day she called me her angel, but sometimes I felt like my horns were holding up my halo!

The purpose of this book is threefold.

First, I want the millions of unpaid caregivers to know that, even though their experiences are unique and personal to them, the journey is a shared one.

Many have experienced or will soon experience the common anguish of unrelenting stress in dealing with the intimate care of a loved one. Hopefully, it helps to know you are not alone, though you may be by yourself. The roller coaster of emotions you are experiencing is perfectly normal. I pray the information in this book will give you the encouragement and validation you need during those times you need it most.

Second, if you anticipate ever needing a caregiver, please begin making provisions and preparations now. Your family and friends will thank you.

Third, if you are not currently a caregiver, please keep reading so you can understand and provide support and encouragement to someone who is.

If you are currently a caregiver, I encourage you to keep a journal, either written or video. It helps with organization for doctor visits, provides a forum for stress relief, improves your own memory, and benefits your own personal health and well-being. It also helps you adjust your own perspective.

My dad passed away several years before my mom's diagnosis of dementia. Early in our journey, Mom was able to stay in her house by herself. Because my brother, Philip, worked in close vicinity to her house, he checked on her during the day, and I stayed on the weekends.

Frequent and multiple daily phone calls and medication monitoring kept her somewhat independent until one sunny spring day when she fell outside and broke her hip. Two angels of mercy "happened" to be driving by, saw her lying on the ground, stopped, and went to her rescue.

My best guess is that one of them stayed with her while the other went into the house and called for an ambulance. Their identities remain a mystery, but our family will always be grateful that they came to my mom's rescue. The ambulance took her to the nearest hospital, but later that day we transferred her to a hospital closer to my house, where she soon had hip-replacement surgery.

The surgery went well, and afterward, she entered a nearby rehabilitation facility to recover. That was quite an experience. On more than one occasion, I had to go to the facility and calm her down so she would go to sleep. One night about 9:00 P.M., Mom was extremely upset, so the nurse called me to come and calm her so she would go to bed. When I arrived at the facility, I found Mom sitting in a wheelchair in the lobby with one shoe on her foot while clutching the other one in her hand. Two aides were attending to her as much as she would let them. She was convinced someone had thrown all of her possessions in the creek. It was her stuff, and she wanted to keep her stuff. Talking to her, using the calmest voice I could find, I convinced her that her stuff was safe and not in the creek. We would straighten out everything in the morning. Finally, she went to bed. I held her hand and soothed her for what seemed like an eternity.

After her two-month stay in rehab, she moved into my house with me. Near the end of her first month's stay, she fell and re-broke her hip while I was out of town, and my brother was on duty. I received the phone call just as I was arriving at my hotel in California for a trip that had been planned for quite some time. Mom had her second emergency surgery, this time while I was out of town. When I returned I drove straight from the airport to the hospital. My brother left, and I was on duty again.

When my mother moved in with me, I had no earthly idea—not an inkling—of how dramatically my life would change.

As you read my journal entries, keep in mind that, originally, I had no intention of publishing any part of this very personal journey. There were some days I did not journal anything. Sleep seemed more important on those nights, and sometimes one day blended into the next. Just because every day is not included, I want you to know that this book contains condensed excerpts from more than five years of journaling everything from Mom's broken hip to the inevitable day of moving her into a long-term care facility.

In May of 2005, I retired from twenty-nine years of teaching junior high school. However, I continued working almost every day substitute teaching at the junior high school from where I retired, so not much really changed as far as going to work every day. Leaving Mom at home on the days I worked certainly had its challenges. Teaching junior high school is where I believe God taught me to develop the patience I would need to live with abundant grace while caring for Mom.

Mother Keys moved in with me on Saturday, June 7, 2008. At first I kept all of the bedroom doors open at night so, in the event Mom needed help, I would hear her call and could assist her. After a while I locked my door at night. I'll explain why later.

Monday, June 9, 2008

At 4:30 A.M. the hall light flashed on. I found Mom at the living room end of the hall, clutching the walls for balance.

"What are you doing? Where are you going?" I quizzed.

She answered, "I don't want to go to the field today. I'm too tired."

We turned around and shuffled slowly back to her room. Oh my gosh! Maybe she had been looking for something. I don't know. In her room I found the blinds open, get well cards scattered on the floor, the walker pushed aside, bedside toilet used and moved, magazine basket kicked aside, and lamp knocked over on to the bed. No lights on! I escorted her back to bed.

Tuesday, June 10, 2008

Tucked Mom in and kissed her good night at 10:15 P.M. the night before. At midnight she was on the bedside toilet. At 2:00 A.M. she was up and using the toilet. At this point I attached a personal alarm to her pajamas so I could get up and help her if she awakened and got out of bed. At 5:00 A.M. I heard the personal alarm sounding. That meant she had moved enough to get out of bed. I rushed in and had some trouble reattaching the alarm to silence it. In the meantime, she had worked her way to the other side of the bed next to the wall. I walked her around the end of the bed and tucked her back in after she used the bedside toilet. Restroom again at 7:00 A.M. Finally awakened her at 9:00 A.M.

Wednesday, June 11, 2008

Put Mom to bed at 10:30 P.M. the night before. Still awake in my room at 11:30 P.M. I heard a noise in the hall. I opened the door, and Mom was dragging her bedside toilet behind her. She asked if she could sleep with me. Of course she could! I set up the toilet on her side by my dresser.

Here was the course of the night. She got up to use the toilet as follows:

12:30 A.M.   1:27 A.M.   3:15 A.M.   5:00 A.M.

At 5:00 A.M. she "regretted sending invitations because I am tired."

No wonder! I let her stay in bed until 9:00 A.M.

Sunday, June 15, 2008—Father's Day

At 3:39 A.M. I spied a shadowy figure in my bedroom doorway. I sprang out of bed to help Mom back to her own. Yes, she was walking without her walker. She said the bed was wet, her panties were soaking wet, and there was a leak in the kitchen.

"Let's take care of it tomorrow," I said. "Let's go back to bed now."

Since her panties were MIA, I put clean ones on her, and then to bed she went. She had used the bedside toilet, the bathroom toilet, and she had put her wet panties in *my* bathroom sink.

Got her up at 8:45 A.M. While taking her sponge bath, she sat on the portable toilet seat in the bathroom. (For some reason, the portable toilet seat had been moved away from the commode and over by the door.) Without warning she crapped all over the floor. Oh my gosh! I remained calm. I finished getting her ready and cleaned her bathroom and the house. My shower felt so good today.

October 22, 2008

As I parked my car in the garage after a long day of teaching junior high students, I smelled it. Burned food. I closed my eyes, said a prayer, took a long, deep breath and slowly counted to ten to calm myself.

I walked into the kitchen. She was standing there looking forlorn. Potatoes were in two separate pots,—one mashed and three single slices in the other one—but the beans were cooked. I walked over and hugged her. She looked relieved. A "hint" of smoke filled the air. Nothing looked burned. What had happened? She had no memory, so she was no help. Stuff was out of place. The cast iron skillet had water in it, and the dish scrubber was totally black, not yellow. Where did the burned food go? Trash? Down the drain? Outside? In the yard? Who knew?

I turned on all exhaust fans and opened the doors to clear out the smoke. We fixed dinner and talked. She didn't remember anything that happened during the day. Didn't even know the nurse had come.

Any Given Sunday—Getting Ready for Church

My sweet Southern Baptist Christian mama dressed up for church every Sunday. That meant dress, hosiery, makeup, and hair. Now, at this stage of the game, trying to put pantyhose on Mom was a very ambitious endeavor. Because of time constraints, I tried helping her. Handing the pantyhose from my hand to hers, I asked her to gather up this leg—meaning the leg of the pantyhose.

As I looked in her closet for clothes she could wear, I didn't pay attention to what she was doing. When I turned around, she had grasped her hands around her right knee and gathered her folded leg close to her chest. She had literally done what I had asked her to do: gathered up her legs! Lying flat on her back with both knees drawn up to her chest, her "nether" region was staring me in the face.

I started laughing so hard I cried. She had no clue. Carefully, and through laughter and tears, I reworded my request, and she complied. From that day forward she wore knee-high hosiery and pants to church.

Getting her ready was such a production that sometimes it did not seem worth the effort.

December 24, 2009

We went to my aunt's house for Christmas Eve and had dinner with her and my cousin. The menu was pizza and salad, and we took some dessert. Mom didn't remember anything about that evening, even on the drive home.

December 31, 2009

We went to a friend's house for a little New Year's Eve celebration. It was very nice. Mom seemed to have a good time. She seemed to enjoy the pleasant conversation even though she didn't contribute. We came home by 10:30 P.M.

January 1, 2010

Mom picked out the black-eyed peas. Good soul food.

February 6, 2010

This had been one of those difficult days.

I had become so very frustrated with my mother's disease. I hated her disease—*not* her. I loved *her* very much. No one was sweeter or kinder than my mother.

That sounds so selfish and petty, but it was how I felt. I was tired of not having my own house. Of not being able to live in my own house and have things my own way, the way I want them to be. I want to put things up and have them stay there, instead of her moving them or me having to move them so she won't break them or lose them.

She had broken so many of my things, many of them gifts from friends: a mantle clock that was a gift from precious friends, a flower vase I received as a retirement gift, a part of my dining table, the lid to my apple dishes sugar bowl, my Hawaiian beanbag doll—and she lost the lid to my favorite travel coffee mug. The list was endless.

She *never* remembered where the dishes went; where the drinking glasses were kept; which plates we used; where the silverware was kept or where to put it up; or where she sat at meals. When I got ready to prepare a meal, I had trouble finding the utensils I needed because she had put them in places that didn't make sense and were always the last places I thought to look. I had become very good at improvising and at hide-and-seek.

She always wanted to help, but wasn't capable. Anything I asked her to do or let her do, I had to be willing to redo or fix.

When I got home from work, I was tired, and I never knew what I would find when I walked in the door. Once, she had taken everything out of the pantry and put it on the table and counters. I was stunned. Oh my gosh! "Mom, did you get bored today?" I asked.

But she didn't have a clue what I was talking about. I put everything back and then fixed dinner. Here is a finite list of sources of infinite frustration for her and for me:

- She ate so very, very slowly.
- She walked/moved ever so slowly.
- Thanked me constantly (which seemed like a good thing, but . . .).
- She constantly wanted to go home (but that home didn't exist anymore).
- "Where is my money?"
- Didn't trust anyone.
- "What about my house? My furniture?"
- "Are my clothes here?"
- She was always cold.
- She hated to take a shower. (It's like giving a cat a bath!)
- She hated to have her hair washed and set. Ironic since she was a retired beautician.

- "Who am I?"
- "Who is my family?"
- "Where are we?"
- "Whose building is this?"
- "Are we going to sleep here tonight?"
- "Do we have any food?"
- "What about my car?"

Sunday, March 13, 2010

Spring forward! Woke up at 10:15 A.M. Mom was already up and fixing toast for breakfast. Later that afternoon I was in my home office working on my taxes. Mom sauntered in, sat down and started asking questions about her house.

"Why can't I live there? Where are we? Where is this house?" You know, the usual. In the midst of answering her questions, she blurted out, "I don't like this place! Why can't I live in my own house?" Shock and dismay hit me like a ton of bricks. Her words hurt my feelings. While trying to keep my emotions in check, there was at least a minute of silence. Then she looked directly at me and said, "I'm listening."

Well, I started crying. Not an ugly cry, but tears were rolling down my face while I was calmly talking to her. In vain I tried to explain why her old house with its falling apart, leaky ceiling, and bathroom floor caving in was not fit to live in, but my explanations were always a practice in futility.

21

My answers did not satisfy her, so she left the room and returned to the living room. It was nearing supper time, and I suggested we eat dinner. I fixed beans and cornbread for her, and I ate a sandwich and beans. While the food was warming, I went to my bathroom and just lost it. Total breakdown. After about a minute, I heard her come to my door and apologize for being rude. I was washing my hands, so I didn't hear everything she said. I told her, "It's okay," but she was already walking away and down the hall.

During our very quiet dinner, we managed some small talk. After dinner she apologized again. I asked her what she was apologizing for, but she didn't know. I asked her how she knew she should apologize. She didn't remember; she just knew. "I don't know what I said, but I just feel like I need to apologize." Of course, I accepted her apology, even though her comment hurt me. I was trying so hard to make a happy home for us. My life had changed also. I, too, had many adjustments to make.

Sunday, June 16, 2010

Mom was feeling a little dizzy in the morning, but nothing out of the ordinary. We were eating breakfast, when suddenly she got up and went to the bathroom. I was sipping my coffee when I heard a crash. My heart nearly stopped; I raced into the bathroom and found her draped face down across the arms of the toilet chair. Her cane had fallen between the tub and the commode.

I grabbed her around the waist and tried to help her up. It was like she was paralyzed. She felt like 135 lbs. of dead weight. While holding her, I tried to move her foot into a more stable position, but I couldn't budge it. Still holding on for dear life, I promised not to let go.

"You won't let me fall will you?" she asked.

I assured her I would not. After what seemed like many minutes, but was probably only a couple, I got her to her feet. She sat down to steady herself. I don't think she blacked out because she didn't end up on the floor. Maybe she tripped over her cane or just lost her balance. Who knew?

Needless to say we didn't make it to church. We stayed home the rest of the day, and she seemed fine. I retrieved both the walker and the wheelchair from the garage and hid her cane. *From this experience I learned to carry my phone with me at all times.*

Monday, June 28, 2010

Yesterday I made my mother cry. Here's what happened:

On Sunday, I got us both up early to shower and do our hair before leaving for church at 10:30 A.M. I had Mom take her "30-minute pill" (she took the pill on an empty stomach and had to wait for thirty minutes before any food or drink) thinking we could get her cleaned up while waiting for coffee and breakfast. Not only did I wake her up early, but she was very, very dizzy and did *not* want to take a shower, and did *not* want to wash her hair. She stood naked in the bathroom and cried, pleading with me not to make her take a shower or wash her hair. I was kind, but firm. Yes, she had to shower and wash her hair. It had been a week since her last shampoo and a couple of days since her last shower. Through tears she tried to assure me one more week would not make any difference. I was sympathetic, but firm. Yes, it would. Her hygiene was important.

Reluctantly and still in tears, she climbed into the tub. I closed the shower curtain for her privacy, and then I leaned against the bathroom wall and sobbed silently. How could I do this to my mother? Because I knew it was for her own good. Even throughout the shower, she kept insisting on not washing her hair. "Sorry, it has to be done."

She survived her shower, so next was her hair. She survived that, too. I rolled it, dried it, and combed it out. Then we had breakfast. Whew! Already a day's work, and it wasn't even 9:30 A.M.! Dizziness was still an issue, but she got dressed. I got dressed. She got very upset that she couldn't find her makeup. It was in the bathroom as always, but she never remembered. Since she was still dizzy, I insisted she take a Dramamine. Okay, so we were made up and ready to go. She made it into the car, and we debated whether we should stay home or go to church. "I guess it would be good for me to go," she said. I suggested, "If you still feel bad when we arrive at church, we can come home." We attended the service and went out to lunch. She was better by this time. Thank you, God.

We came home. I cleaned house and prepared for company. Some of my friends came with food to share for dinner. It was a lovely evening. Mom stayed and fellowshipped with us.

Monday, June 28, 2010

This morning at 7:30 A.M. Mom greeted me with, "I shit all over the house! I don't think I made it to the bathroom in time." Oh my word! At this point I want you to know my saintly mother never before used off-color or inappropriate language. *Ever.* That being said, I calmly went to investigate. Not too bad. As a matter of fact, she had made it to the bathroom, put her soiled underwear and pajama bottoms on the bathroom counter, and had already put on clean undies and had on a robe. I put her back to bed, and I cleaned the bathroom. She slept until almost 10:00 A.M. When she got up, we had breakfast, and she took a shower with no argument. Praise the Lord!

Thursday, July 1, 2010

Last night Noma called me, and we chatted for a while as we always did. When I came back to the living room, Mom asked who had called, and I told her it was Noma.

She said, "Noma. She calls Debbie sometimes, too."

"Who is Debbie?"

"My daughter."

I asked, "Who am I?"

"I don't know. My daughter?"

At 3:00 A.M. my door opened, and Mom came in because she didn't know if it was day or night and thought she was there alone. I loudly told her (the volume required no hearing aids) to go back to bed. She was looking for the bathroom located literally four steps from her room. I got up and discovered the living room light was on, as was the light in her room, and she was wandering around trying to find the bathroom. I turned off the living room light, waited for her to get finished in the bathroom, and put her back in bed. She apologized profusely, and said, "I am such a problem." I assured her she was not a problem. She went back to sleep, and I stayed awake for two more hours.

Sunday, July 11, 2010

Once again, late to church. She wouldn't wear what I picked out for her, so for the second or third Sunday in a row, she wore the same dress. It drove me crazy. I knew it was not a big deal, but it was one of many, many, *many* little deals!

She washed dishes after lunch, and I went to my home office to work for a while.

She put the dishes away in the cabinets after they were dry—and paced like a caged animal, walking around the house for "exercise."

At dinnertime when I looked in the cabinet to get the dishes, they were all in the wrong places. I attempted to rearrange them so they would fit. Well, I dropped two small bowls of my apple dishes. I screamed out loud, thinking at the same time *if they had been put up correctly, I wouldn't have had to rearrange them. I wouldn't have dropped them and broken them.* Oh well, they would just have to join the other apple dishes in apple-dish heaven. It was getting crowded up there!

Mom tried to help, but I was afraid she would fall over as she bent at the waist to pick the pieces up off of the floor. I yelled at her to stop. She argued. I yelled again. In a tone of dejection, she said, "Okay, I'll just go over here and sit down." I felt like a heel! I swept up the pieces of broken dishes, returned the broom to the utility room, leaned on the dryer, and silently sobbed. Tears fell into a puddle on the dryer. I prayed, "God, if you don't help me, I am going to lose it." I was at my wit's end.

Dinner was pretty quiet, except for her questions about her money and checks. Again. I kept telling her I knew why Dad had called her the "DA." She had more questions than a five year old. And she asked the same ones over and over and over *and over* again. For four-and-a-half solid hours, every five minutes, she asked the same questions about her money, her mail, her house, her car, and her clothes. Each time she asked, my tone became sharper and more curt. I even began praying out loud as I sat beside her on the couch holding her hand and trying to answer her questions. I just felt so very bad about my attitude. I didn't know what to do or how to handle it. Answering the same questions over and over again was maddening. I just couldn't seem to control the tone of my responses. My frustration came through with every answer I gave her.

Finally it was time for bed. Mom had to wear a pad for incontinence, but sometimes thought it was for her period and said she only needed to wear the pad for two or three days a month. She had a hysterectomy in 1971, so no chance of that!

Just as she was about to lie down on the bed, somehow the pad got out of position. She tried to reposition it, but was having trouble.

"Well, shit!" she said out loud.

"That's pretty much how I feel about it," I said. We had a good laugh. Me through my tears. It had been a very rough day.

Thursday, July 22, 2010

It was midnight. Mom was up and wanting to go outside to get the boy with the horse.

"Mom, there is no boy here and no boy with a horse."

"Yes, there is!"

"No, it's midnight."

"I can't leave that boy out there," she insisted.

"There is no boy and no horse."

"I feel terrible leaving him. Go with me."

"This is a residential area, not the country. It's midnight, and I'm not going outside with you. Let's sit down and talk."

Finally, after fifteen minutes, I convinced her to lie down and go back to bed.

Wednesday, October 27, 2010

I was sitting on the couch right beside her. She said, "You know, my family hasn't called to check on me in a while."

Going along with her, I responded, "Who is your family?"

"My children," she stated without hesitation.

I couldn't resist. "Why, those evil children! Who are your children?"

"Well, there's Philip, Mitchell, Brent, Trevor and . . . a girl."

"A girl? Debbie?" (I didn't mention that Mitchell, Brent, and Trevor were actually her grandsons—and my nephews.)

"Yes, Debbie."

"Where does Debbie live?"

"In Dallas somewhere."

"Hellooo . . . Why do you think I call you Mama?"

"Are you my daughter?" She seemed surprised.

"Yes, it's me. Debbie."

"I'm sorry. I keep forgetting that."

January 2-3, 2011

Mom went to bed at 10:15 P.M. Again, up at midnight. I found her standing in the shower, facing the wall. I convinced her to go back to bed. She was up again at 2:47 A.M. She was in the living room. How in the world did she find her way there in the dark? She refused to go back to bed, wouldn't go into her room, and didn't want to go outside—not that I would have suggested that she go outside. She was very upset and agitated. After trying to get her back to bed by talking sternly and loudly (so she could hear me with no hearing aids), I heard these words come out of my mouth. "Get your butt back in this bed!"

I guess she took me seriously because she slowly began to saunter back to her room. She cried, and I cried as we sat on the side of her bed. She couldn't be consoled. I didn't know what to do. I just put my arms around her and held her. Finally, she lay down, but when she closed her eyes, she clenched them shut so tightly that she made a face. I lay down beside her. She wouldn't talk or open her eyes. When some time had passed, I went back to my bed and cried myself to sleep . . . again.

Friday, March 11, 2011

At 6:00 A.M. a banging sound was coming from some other room in the house. I got up to investigate and found Mom standing in the kitchen at the utility room door. I wasn't sure if she had been banging on the inside or outside door to the garage. Did it really matter?

"Mom, what are you doing?"

"I can't get out of this house!" she shouted, her tone frustrated.

"It's 6:00 in the morning. Why don't you go back to bed?"

"Well, I have to go the bathroom."

"Okay, it's on the way. Let's go." I gently coaxed her back to bed by way of the bathroom.

Again at 7:15 A.M. a banging sound came from some other room in the house. I got up to investigate and found Mom standing in the kitchen at the utility room door . . . same scenario as before, except this time she was "freezing her butt off!,"—and she had on pants over her pajama bottoms.

When Mom awoke at 8:30 A.M., she was totally unaware of the goings-on of the past two-and-half hours. Breakfast was eggs, toast, and coffee. I made her take a shower. She had a hair appointment at 11:00, and she was not happy about that.

While picking up her room, I spied a flower vase from a table in the living room sitting on the floor by her dresser. I was very puzzled and wondered why she would move it into her room. I thought, *Gosh, I hope she didn't pee in it.* I quickly dismissed that thought.

I got her clothes ready for after her shower. That done, I went to return the vase to the living room, and could not believe what I found. Lo and behold, she *had* peed in the vase! I found no evidence that she had peed on the carpet. I was even more puzzled now because I didn't know if she sat down and aimed carefully, if she put the vase in the chair and sat on it, or maybe she held it up to herself and emptied that little bladder.

Anyway, I lost it. I was crying, mad, frustrated, upset, and even a little bit amused . . . you name it, I went through a gamut of emotions. I felt like this was the last straw. Flowers for my retirement reception were sent to me in that vase. Was nothing sacred? I emptied the pee into my toilet and put the vase in my shower promising myself to clean it later. I couldn't face it at that moment.

Wednesday, June 1, 2011

Up early before 6:00 A.M. for work. I heard Mom get up, so I checked on her. She was in the kitchen trying to find that elusive bathroom. I guided her back to her room. She took her pills, went to the bathroom, then back to bed. *That was smooth*, I thought.

About five minutes later, a little knock on my bedroom door. Questions about the house, where we live, was there food, was there a phone, a kitchen, a bathroom . . . etc. I took her on a short tour of the house. She headed back to bed, and I was left to get ready. Five minutes later, a little knock on my door. Questions . . . same scene. Five minutes later, a little knock on my door. Questions . . . same scene.

Finally, she went back to bed, and I went off to work. Work . . . haircut . . . back home.

Mom met me at the garage door. "You are an angel. I was wondering if anybody was coming to get me. I don't like being here in this house by myself." I hugged her and told her, "I love you." She was very relieved I was home. For some reason she was wearing my blouse. Didn't have a clue why. Apparently, she just went to my closet, took it off the hanger and put it on. I asked her, "Why are you wearing my blouse?" She felt bad and went immediately to change it. However, instead, she took off her jacket and hung it in my closet. She put my blouse on her chair in her room. She couldn't remember what was mine, but she knew something was.

At dinner, she knocked over her glass full of water. It went everywhere—the table, the floor, our placemats—*everywhere*. Somehow I kept my cool. I cleaned it up, and we continued eating dinner.

We watched a little television, and then it was time for pajamas. Three times she went in to finish putting on her pajamas. Pajama top on, but she still had her pants on from the day. Whew! Same questions all night long which made watching television very difficult. Money, bank, mail, whose house? . . . Money, bank, mail, whose house? . . . I became so tired.

Friday, June 17, 2011

I opened my bedroom door to leave for my two-mile walk in the morning, and a chair from my office was blocking the doorway. *What in the world?* I moved the chair back to its proper location and left for my walk. I returned and waited for Mom to get up. At about 8:45 A.M. she opened her door, and I discovered she had moved the chair into her room. She was so strong and active during the night. I don't know how she managed to move that heavy chair between her dresser and bed and turn it around. No clue!

After a cup of coffee and a bowl of cereal, I got her to take a shower, and then I took her to her hair appointment. Always a battle. She didn't want to go, but her hair looks and lasts so much better when Carla does it. We came home and had lunch. We rested for a while and then went to the grocery store. Oh my gosh! Bless her heart, she gets around so very, very slowly. She asked the same questions all day long. Sorry to say I didn't handle it very well today. Some days are better than others. I spent much of the day returning her cane to her.

Sunday, June 19, 2011—Father's Day

Oh my gosh! At 4:30 A.M. I was startled awake by loud banging on my locked bedroom door. *Mom!* I got up, answered the door and found her so disoriented and confused (more than usual). "I can't get out of here! How do I get out of here? Did she go home?" and many other insane questions. She couldn't find that elusive bathroom either. I not-so-nicely escorted her to the bathroom, then back to her room. She wasn't happy to go, but as soon as she realized she had awakened me from a deep sleep (which wasn't difficult to discern, judging from my crabbiness), she apologized profusely. "I'm sorry. I'm sorry." I tucked her back in, turned off all of the lights she had turned on, and went back to bed. After a long while, I finally went back to sleep.

When I got up between 8:15 and 8:30 A.M., Mom was already up. I went in to get a cup of coffee and lo and behold, she had *unplugged* the coffee pot *and* its timer. I silently burst into tears, trying to hide my face from Mom as she sat at the table waiting for breakfast. After a tiring night, I had been so looking forward to a hot cup of fresh coffee, but the entire pot of coffee . . . *cold*! I was *so* frustrated and angry. Not at Mom, but at her disease. I made a fresh pot of coffee.

We had breakfast, she took a shower, and I got her ready for church. God knew I needed to go. I got ready, loaded Mom and her walker into the car, and off we went in my 1999 Mercury Mountaineer. She was getting so very slow. The process was now taking at least three times longer than it used to take.

Mexican food was our restaurant of choice. Philip called to accept my invitation for lunch at my house, but too late. We were almost finished eating at the restaurant, so we went home to rest and read the paper. We had an outing to Bath and Body Works for the final day of the sale. The wind was so strong, it almost blew Mom away. I shopped quickly so as not to tire her out. She followed me around the store like a puppy. Bless her heart.

Whenever we went for a drive, Mom always asked what town we were in, and no matter what I would tell her, she always said, "It is really spread out" and "This is a well-kept area." These were *always* her responses.

Money questions . . . "When am I going home?" . . . "Can I spend the night?" . . . "Where is my bed?" . . . "Where is the potty?"—these questions were on our agenda for the rest of the night, *every* night.

Tuesday, June 21, 2011

"I will be glad when somebody takes me home. I don't like it here."

I knew in my head she hadn't meant it the way I took it. I fired back, "I'm sorry, Mom. I try to make a happy home here for us. I'm doing the best I can."

"Oh is this your house?" she asked, looking confused.

"Yes. You've been here for over three years."

"Well, I just miss being in my own house. I didn't mean to be rude. Thank you for taking care of me."

I assured her everything was okay, then I went to the other room and cried. I was so frustrated with myself. Why couldn't I just blow it off anymore? I didn't want to take her comments personally, but they still hurt every time.

Wednesday, June 22, 2011

I got up early and took my forty-minute walk. After the early morning rain, the weather was wonderful. When I returned home, I took a shower and had coffee. While I was sitting on the sofa eating cereal, Mom sneaked in behind me, clapped her hands and announced, "I need your help."

"How can I help you?"

"I need you to help me go see this lady so I can tell her my husband left me, and I don't have any money!"

"So, when did your husband leave you?" I asked.

"Oh a couple of weeks . . . a couple of months ago."

"Well, I'm your daughter, and your husband and my father passed away several years ago. So, he did leave you, but he went to heaven."

"I didn't get married again?" she asked.

"Not that I know of."

"Well . . . that's some tough stuff! I better sit down before I fall down."

We began laughing so loudly and heartily! Even Mom seemed to realize the absurdity of this story. She was really laughing out loud.

Sunday, July 10, 2011

Worst day ever. Okay, maybe not the worst, but certainly among the top ten. The day started when Mom got up at 4:00 A.M., turned on the lights and tried to escape, first through the front door, and then the back door. I got up to check on her, and she wanted me to help her contact a woman because she couldn't watch the woman's little boy today. I hugged her and explained that there was no little boy, and that it was four o'clock in the morning. I tried to get her back to bed, and she went reluctantly. She went back to sleep, and, of course, I was awake for hours.

Well, we didn't go to church, and I'm really sorry about that. There was just too much to do to get ready. Mom needed a shower, her hair washed and set, in addition to getting her dressed for church. I had to shower and get dressed myself. She needed to take one of her pills that required an empty stomach for thirty minutes, and then we would need to eat breakfast. Just too overwhelming.

The constant questioning and having to answer those questions over and over and over again brought on so much stress. "Do I get any money? Where is my money? Can I get my money? Whose building is this? Where is this house? Where's my family? Are we going to sleep here? Do I have a bed here? Do we have any food?" . . . and more. I felt like she was always on my last good nerve. Every time she asked a question, her mind seemed to think she was asking for the first time. My mind told me it was the 3,217th time she had asked!

Mom went to the bathroom every twenty to thirty minutes. A mystery. I tried to get her to wait, but she insisted. I always had to show her the way. Every single time.

The vegetable sprayer had a leak, so the cabinet under the sink was all wet. Tried duct tape, but it was not the best solution. Mom spilled water on the table during dinner. The ice maker in the refrigerator/freezer has a water leak that needs to be repaired. Tons of laundry to do. Mom was restless and was wandering around. Computer was so, so slow.

I became so tired of maintenance.

Monday, July 11, 2011

Mom had an appointment with Dr. Vengalil at 10:30 A.M. We arrived, checked in, and waited briefly, then were called back to the exam room. Everyone was very nice. I mentioned a few issues to Dr. Vengalil (bumps on chest, earwax, constant bathroom visits). Bumps were not serious, but the other issues required procedures.

Mom went with the nurse to give a urine sample. She not only had to "void," but also had a bowel movement. Needless to say no urine sample was taken at this time. The nurse asked me if Mom was getting worse, if she seemed more confused. "Yes," I replied, "but sometimes it's hard to tell." Mom and the nurse returned to the exam room. Time for the ear cleaning. Oh, fun. The nurse explained what she was going to do. Like that would help. I knew she had to say it, though. After a couple of squirts in Mom's ear with the syringe, Mom yelled, "ouch." The nurse persisted, but

Mom kept yelling "ouch," and this scene was repeated a number of times with both ears.

As the nurse cleaned out her ears, Mom yelled many, many times, "Let's just cut it off! Just cut it off!" Now, she meant to stop the procedure, not to actually cut off her ear. Boy, did the nurse get stuff out of her ears, much to Mom's discomfort. I was laughing so hard I was crying—and totally embarrassed that Mom was frightening other patients.

On the way out, Mom could finally give a urine sample, tiny as it was, but enough to test for a UTI (and yes, she had one).

On the way home, Mom couldn't remember the ordeal. So strange. We went by Walgreens, got the Rx, went home, and had lunch. Whew!

Sunday, July 17, 2011

It had been a fairly "normal" day for us. At some point during the afternoon, Mom went to the bathroom and then to her room. When she was walking back up the hall, I met her and hugged her and asked her, "How are you?"

She told me she had been to the potty and to her room looking around. She said, "I saw the bed and said, 'I'll be there soon.' And the bed said to me, 'Hurry up.'"

We laughed a lot. Sitting on the couch, she asked, "Did I just arrive today?"

"No, you've lived here more than three years."

"Not in my mind," she said. "I was at my mother's house today, and walked up and down the road both ways."

I told her, "Maybe in Derleneland, but in the real world we got up, had breakfast and went to church. Then, we came home, had lunch, bought a paper, read it and relaxed today." I told her it must be nice to take a trip any time she wanted.

She said, "Yes, I like it that way." Just another day in the life . . .

Wednesday, July 27, 2011

Joyous day! My great niece was born this morning at 7:52 A.M. weighing in at 7 lbs., 10 oz., 20 ½ inches. Sweetest, most adorable little girl in the world.

I helped Mom get ready, and we went to the hospital to meet our newest little blessing. I got to hold her for a while. Precious. Tears of joy were silently streaming down my face. I was overcome. Really missed Dad today. He would have loved to meet this precious gift from God.

Mom asked the same questions many times: "Is it a boy or a girl? What's her name? Whose baby is she?"

But Mom did okay today.

Thursday, July 28, 2011

After preparing breakfast for Mom and me, I ran some errands. Came back home to Mom. We had lunch. I answered the same questions over and over. She was concerned about her memory and guessed the Lord must not be ready for her yet. When I was tucking her in bed tonight, she asked once more how long she had lived here. I told her more than three years. She didn't remember and said I must be asking the Lord to release me from this duty. We laughed. I said, "Yes, I ask the Lord to 'Please release me from this duty'—not!" Kissed her good night, told her I loved her.

Friday, July 29, 2011

First the shower, then getting dressed, then the struggle to go to the beauty shop. I took her "kicking and screaming." She never wanted to go, but eventually would give in, usually as we walked into the salon.

I left her with Carla, then I went to the hospital to see my niece and brand-spanking-new great-niece. Oh my gosh! She was so adorable—the most precious child alive. (The unbiased opinion of a great aunt.) I got to hold the precious new baby for a long time. It was so wonderful and refreshing. After soaking up as much new baby essence as I could, I went to retrieve Mom, and we came home for lunch. I went to the grocery store and back. Since Mom seemed to be doing okay, I left her at home, and I went to get my haircut and to another grocery store. Shopping the sales. Had to pinch pennies.

Then the day took quite a turn.

While filling my grocery cart, my cell phone started ringing like crazy. The alarm company called about my house alarm going off. Twice. Once at 5:24 P.M. and again at 5:26 P.M. They called all three people on my alarm security list, and in turn, those three people all called me. In the checkout line of the grocery store, I explained to each one that Mom was home and had probably inadvertently set off the alarm. Since the alarm company couldn't reach me, they dispatched the police. On the way home, I called the police and tried to cancel the dispatch, but only the alarm company could do that.

I sped the two miles to my home, pulled into the garage, flung the car door open, turned the car off, but left the keys in the ignition. I ran into the house to find the front door open and Mom standing in her housecoat, looking quite forlorn and frightened. She was very upset. Of course, so was I. I knew better, but I asked, "What happened?"

"I don't know why that thing was going off. It was nothing I did. It's not my fault."

As I was on the house phone clearing up the mess with the alarm company, a city police car pulled up in front of my house. I hung up with the alarm people and met the policeman at the door. I explained the situation as I was escorting Mom back into the cool house. July was so hot—all she needed was a heatstroke. The police officer didn't seem very interested in my explanation. As a matter of fact, he appeared quite distracted.

He said, "Do you know you have a snake right there by your front door?" No wonder he was ignoring me. He was trying to avoid a snakebite! Neither of us knew what kind of snake it was. I suggested calling animal control. He tried, but it was after hours. No one would be there until Monday. He didn't have anything in his car that would help, so he left. Nice, but not very helpful.

I still hadn't quite calmed down from the alarm, and now I was dealing with a snake by my front door. I went back inside, and Mom was still very upset. "I'm disgusted," she said. "And I want to go home. I hate this place! I hate being blamed for something I didn't do."

By the grace of God, I remained very calm. I held her hands and spoke to her in a soothing voice, reassuring her she was fine; nothing was her fault. Then she tried to blame everything on the snake! I laughed.

I called Philip for advice and texted him pictures of the snake. Not very close-up ones, though. He said to get a hoe or shovel and kill it.

"What if it chases me?" I asked.

"It won't chase you," Philip said. "And if it does, you can outrun a snake!"

"Have you *seen* me run? No! Because I don't run!"

"Get some wasp or hornet spray so you can spray from far away."

To avoid any more alarm situations, I loaded Mom into the car, and we drove to Dollar General. She stayed in the car while I went inside to purchase wasp spray. As I stood in line to check out, I tried to convince the guy behind me to come to my house and kill the snake! He just laughed. He said, "It's probably a chicken snake."

We came back home. The moment of truth had arrived. I had to put my "big girl panties" on and handle the situation.

After much earnest prayer, I emptied that can (from a safe distance) on that snake, then very quickly grabbed the shovel and chopped it! Oh my gosh! That little sucker was over three feet long!

Upon its demise I texted a much more up-close picture to Philip, and he assured me it was a chicken snake. I said, "A bigger chicken killed it!"

I had been planning on having tacos for dinner, but the taco shells were MIA. I think Mom either ate them or hid them. I was at the end of my rope. She had a sandwich, and I had a taco filling without the shell, which would be a taco salad.

Just another day in the life.

Saturday, July 30, 2011

Not a bad day until the dryer quit working. It would tumble, but there was no heat. Oh, great. I washed our clothes, but had to go to the laundromat to dry some of them. I hung some clothes on a clothesline in the garage to dry, then headed out. Of course, I took Mom with me. On the way to the laundromat, I noticed my car was not cooling very well. Oh, great. Again. Dryer wouldn't heat, and the car wouldn't cool. The sink sprayer hose was leaking, too, which had damaged the cabinet under the sink. And my fridge was collecting water at the bottom by the bucketful. Mom had lost her left hearing aid. I was leaving town in the morning and by 11:00 P.M., had not yet packed. Not sure how much more of this I could handle—I really needed this upcoming short break.

Sunday, September 4, 2011

Much has happened since my last entry.

Today was not a bad day. Not like earlier in the week when I returned home from work and found cereal all over the table and in various containers around the kitchen. Most of the jelly Mom tried to eat had come to rest on her left pant leg and on random places in the kitchen.

Back to today . . . I helped Mom install her incontinence pad earlier in the evening. Whew, got that done. Foolish me! Later while I was helping her with her pajamas, I found she had removed the pad and put it on her nightstand. After a short outburst on my part regarding pad #2, I put her to bed after three trips to the bathroom in twenty minutes. At the third trip, nothing came out. Her going to the restroom every twenty to thirty minutes didn't bother me, it was her needing directions to the bathroom every time she went.

I tucked her into bed.

"Thank you for having patience with me," she said.

"I'm not sure I do," I answered.

"Oh, yes, you do, or I would be out the door. Bye!" she said, waving her arm.

I started cracking up at this point. Kissed her goodnight and closed the door. I took her hearing aids to the kitchen to store them, and checked her pill cup. By George, she still had two pills she hadn't taken. She always wanted to save them to take later. She believed there were so many pills they might get confused as to what to do. Really? I marched right back into her room, pills and water in hand, turned on the light, and gave her the pills to take. Usual discussion about taking pills ensued. I ranted about having to "watch her take every single pill from now on."

She looked straight up at me, right in the eye, and said, "I have a mental problem!"

I laughed hard at this point. So did Mom.

"I know," I finally said.

"I don't have to tell you," Mom said. "I need to go to the potty."

"You just went three times. Nothing came out the third time, and you said you would believe me the next time."

"Well, I guess if I have to go, I'll just wet the bed."

"You can't wet the bed. You don't have any pee left! Nothing will come out!"

Through our laughter, we both said, "Love you. Good night."

Tuesday, September 6, 2011

Before I left for work, I awakened Mom to take her pills, helped her change her pad, then go to the bathroom. While she was sitting on the toilet, I went to get her pills, and when I returned she looked very upset. "Are you okay?" I asked.

"I'm horrible!"

"What's the matter?"

"They put me in jail!"

"What did you do?" I asked, stunned.

"I don't know, but they won't let me go."

"Mom, you are not in jail. You are in my house. Why don't you take your pills and go back to bed."

"They won't let me go anywhere," she said, pouting.

"You are okay. Just go back to bed, and you'll be fine."

"Okay."

She was not happy about it, but she went back to bed, and I went to work.

Thursday, Sept. 8, 2011

I got up early and went for a walk. When I returned, Mom was still asleep, so I let her stay in bed until about 9:30 A.M. She got up and asked about the two little boys we were watching. "Did somebody come and get the little boys?"

Instead of clarifying or correcting her, I replied, "Yes. Would you like some coffee?"

She went to the bathroom. Oh my gosh! I wasn't prepared for what happened next. After a minute I checked on her. She forgot to flush the toilet, so I attempted to flush it for her. There was so much excrement in the commode that it looked like she took a laxative and exploded into the toilet. I also noticed she had deposited her incontinence pad, fully absorbed by this time, into the commode. If she had flushed . . . I shudder to think about the cost of the plumbing bill due to all that overflow!

Not only was the commode full, but there were "deposits" on the arm of the toilet chair, on the cabinet above the toilet paper, on the floor . . . you name it. I immediately put her in the shower while I cleaned the bathroom.

Her shower a distant memory, I got her dressed, and we ate breakfast. Next struggle—beauty shop. She hated to go, and I told her she could gripe and complain all she wanted to, but she was going.

Thursday, September 22, 2011

Working every day and leaving Mom at home alone took a toll on her. She became more confused, didn't eat right during the day, and became dehydrated and even more restless. Before leaving for work, I woke her up and had her take her pills, changed her pad and her clothes, kissed her goodbye, and put her back to bed.

Good day at school, now home. When I drove down the alley, I looked in the backyard as I always did. Through the fence I could see that the back door was wide open. Strange. I backed the car into the garage and noticed that the door from the garage into the house was also wide open. Panic set in when I saw the front door was wide open. I ran into the house yelling, "Mom!" No answer. "Mom!" No answer. Racing through the house, "MOM!" No answer. Deeper panic. Where was she? Had someone kidnapped her? The walker was missing, but her cane was in place. Had she run away from home? As I sped through the house, I called Philip. "I can't find your mother!" He was on his way.

I drove the neighborhood searching for any sign of her or her walker. Neither was anywhere to be found. Talked to my neighbor across the street. She hadn't seen her. Oh my gosh! What happened to her? Where could she be?

I returned home and called the police to report my missing mother.

"She is here at the station," an officer told me. "A citizen found her and called the police."

"I will be right there!" I said, then called Philip.

Composed and grateful she was safe, I drove straight to the station, parked, and emerged from my car. Two officers and a woman were standing beside a patrol car, its front door open. The officer asked, "Are you here to pick up your mother?"

"Yes," I answered.

Mom was sitting in the front seat of the patrol car. When our eyes met, I started crying. The woman stepped in front of me to block Mom's view. The officer then asked me to step to the side so I could gain my composure. "Yes, I have to calm down," I said. He gave me a clipboard with a form on it. Since I was in no condition to fill out paperwork at that time, he let me take it with me if I promised to bring it back "in case we have to do this again."

After gaining composure, I went to the police car, leaned in and hugged Mom. I asked her, "How are you?"

"Horrible." She was very upset.

I tried to comfort her and told her we would go home and have a nice dinner and talk about our day.

She was ready. Mom asked, "Do we need to pay any money to get out of here?"

We all laughed. "No, we don't have to bail you out of jail, Mom." More laughter.

Slowly, and with assistance, Mom emerged from the squad car and shuffled to my car.

The very kind officer loaded the walker into the back of my SUV. I thanked them all profusely, and Mom and I took off for home. Mom didn't remember any of the day's events on the way home and was appalled when I related her adventure to her.

I called Philip on the way home, relaying Mom had wandered away from home, a citizen had found her, and called the police. I soon learned the citizen was a female Dallas police officer. I arrived home with my little runaway in tow. We had a nice dinner. Mom couldn't figure out why she was so tired. I called my cousin, and she agreed to stay with Mom for a couple of days while I worked.

Monday, December 19, 2011

We got ready and went to a longtime family friend's house for a church Christmas party. Everyone was so very thrilled to see Mom. They welcomed her with open arms. She acted as though she knew them, and probably recognized almost everyone at the time, but had no recollection later.

Tuesday, January 3, 2012 (My birthday)

For the last two months, Mom has been declining mentally and physically. She has become confused, disoriented, stooped, slower, and dizzy.

At one point she couldn't remember how to go to the bathroom, or where to sit, or what to do. One day she was willing to do the dishes, but she didn't know what to do. I had to show her. She was willing to fold clothes, just not sure how to do that either.

So this morning I awakened at 1:47 A.M. and couldn't go back to sleep. Tossed and turned and watched TV until about 4:00 A.M. About 4:20 A.M. I finally drifted back to sleep. At 4:41 A.M. Mom rattled my doorknob and woke me up trying to enter my room. Man, I had just gone back to sleep! I got up and put her back to bed after she went to the bathroom. I went back to bed, but not back to sleep until about 6:30 A.M. So tired.

A dear friend called, and we made lunch plans. I decided to get showered and dressed before Mom got up. As soon as I got out of the shower, I heard the door chime from the alarm. *Why is she going outside?* I put on some clothes and went looking for her. She wasn't in her room, or in her bathroom. She wasn't in the living room or kitchen or utility room. Outside doors were locked from the inside. Then I thought, *the garage!*

There she was wandering around looking for the bathroom. After conversation and questioning, I got her back inside to the bathroom and back to bed. She had to get up before I left so I could get her breakfast, get her dressed, and set for the day.

My sweet friend treated me to birthday lunch at Chili's. Next to Chili's was Corner Bakery, so I bought a baby Bundt cake for my birthday. I did some shopping and came on home.

I found only a few things awry. Mayo lid on the peanut butter jar and the peanut butter lid on the mayo jar. They were both out of the fridge and on the counter. A can of cranberry sauce out of the pantry and in a cabinet on the opposite wall. Who knew why?

Wanting Mom to get some activity every day, we went to Dollar General to walk around. Came back home, received some birthday phone calls, then went to Sonic to get half-priced hamburgers for dinner. Did I know how to celebrate or what?

On the way back we were talking about it being my birthday. I said to Mom, "Just think, Mom, fifty-nine years ago today somebody was yelling at you saying, 'Push!'"

She laughed and laughed. Then she took my hand and said the sweetest words, "That's the best thing that ever happened to me . . . having you." My eyes filled with happy tears.

We ate our hamburgers at home, and then after dinner, I lit the candles on the baby Bundt cake and made Mom sing to me.

"Happy birthday to you. Happy birthday to you. Happy birthday, dear . . . " She couldn't remember my name.

"Who am I?"

"I don't remember your name. I don't even remember who I am!"

"It's Debbie. I'm your daughter."

"Dear Debbie . . . happy birthday to you."

We blew out the candles and enjoyed some cake and ice cream.

Got ready for bed. She always wanted to go outside to go to the "potty." I reminded her there was one inside now.

Wednesday, January 18, 2012

At 7:00 A.M. I woke up Mom for potty, pills, and pad. Two out of three wasn't bad. Where was the pad? Oh, it was on the bathroom floor next to the potty chair. At least it wasn't down the toilet. Mission accomplished. Mom back to bed.

After work, I came through the back door into the kitchen from the garage as usual. "Hellooo, I'm home." A quick inventory of the room revealed Mom's walker in place and the front door locked from the inside. Ah, she hadn't escaped! She was in the house. Her bathroom door was almost closed. I peeked in. Bless her heart. She was sitting on the toilet, badly soiled panties in her left hand, shit on the floor, jeans on the counter, pajama top on, and a forlorn look on her face. At least the shit was contained to the bathroom. And I mean shit . . . literally.

Oh my gosh! She couldn't figure out what had happened. She knew something had happened, but didn't know what. I assumed "clean up" mode. Made Mom strip and get into the tub. Made her take a long shower, twice! She had shit all over her—legs, butt, and hands. She looked so pathetic. My heart just broke for her. While she showered, I cleaned the bathroom. Where to start? Thank God for disposable disinfectant sheets. Must have used an entire container. Threw away the panties. Well, what did we have there? The incontinence pad? In the toilet? Five times its normal size? Soaked up almost all of the water in the bowl! Oh my gosh! Thank God she didn't try to flush it. Plumbing bill would have been sky high. After the disinfectant sheets, I bleached the bathroom floor and everything within its walls. I, of course, was wearing rubber gloves!

After her shower I opened the curtain, gave Mom a towel to dry off with, and she couldn't remember anything that had happened. Unbelievable!

Despite the challenges of the day, the rest of the evening went well, even with the repetition of the same few questions. Mom got ready for bed by herself for a change. As far as conversations went, she was really having trouble with word choices. Her reasoning and verbal skills were suffering and diminishing. Sometimes I really did not understand what she was trying to say. She became as frustrated as I did. Maybe more so.

As I was tucking her in at bedtime, she asked, as she often did, "Am I the only one sleeping in this bed tonight?"

I answered, "Well, yes, unless you have someone I don't know about."

"Well, maybe I'll just sneak them in."

Asking for clarification, I said, "Them or him?"

"Or maybe I'll just sneak out with them!"

Laughter filled the room. Good way to end a very trying day.

Wednesday, January 25, 2012

At 2:43 A.M. there was banging on my bedroom door. I was jarred out of a dead sleep. Mom! I opened my door to a very frightened little mama. Somehow I found my calm, soothing voice. "What's wrong?"

"I want to come into the house!"

"You are in the house."

"No, I'm not. I want to come into the house."

I maneuvered Mom back to her room, all the while reassuring her she was in the house. She just got lost. We sat on the side of the bed, and she said, "It looks like y'all would let an old woman like me in the house!"

While stifling a chuckle and still using the calmest voice I could muster, I reassured her that she was in the house.

After she went to the potty, I tucked her in, told her I loved her and to go back to sleep. She apologized over and over. "No problem," I said. "I had to get up to answer my door anyway."

Saturday, January 28, 2012

After our morning activities, Mom relaxed on the sofa. She was a little chilled, so I gave her a lap blanket to wrap up in. She put it around her shoulders and over her head. I was standing behind her and asked, "Mom?"

She started laughing and said, "Did you think I had disappeared?"

I cracked up. "Yes, I thought you had on a cloak of invisibility!"

We laughed so hard.

Sunday, January 29, 2012

At 1:47 A.M. I heard knocking on a distant door. The utility room door? The door to the garage? "Mom?"

I got up to investigate and found her wandering around in the living room. Again, I used my calm, soothing voice. "Mom, what are you doing?"

"I had to sleep in the car!"

"You what?"

"I had to sleep in the car! I couldn't get into the house."

"You are in the house. Let's go back to bed."

"I have to get the groceries. There are groceries in the car."

"Mom, I'll get the groceries. Why don't you just go back to bed?"

"I have to go to the potty."

"Okay then, let's go back to bed. It's 2:00 in the morning."

I tucked her in. Some time passed, and she was up again. I guided her back to bed. Again, some time passed, and she was up again. I guided her back to bed, and she slept until almost 10:00 A.M., but I got up at 7:30 A.M. Whew!

Tuesday, January 31, 2012

I could hear her snoring through the closed bedroom door. I hated to wake her up when she was sleeping so soundly. I entered her room quietly and gently rubbed her arm. She awoke and mumbled, "Goodnight."

"It's morning." I replied.

"Oh . . . do I have to go to work?" Mom asked, still groggy.

"No, you don't have to work anymore. You've retired."

"I did? From what?"

"You were a hairdresser for a long time. Now you are retired."

"How do I get money?"

"You paid into Social Security when you were working, and now it's paying you back." Here I was explaining Social Security benefits at 6:55 A.M. to a woman with dementia.

Mom inexplicably burst out laughing. She laughed for a good thirty seconds. Caught me completely off guard, but I just went with it and laughed, too. With hands pressed together as if in prayer, she exclaimed, "Well, praise the Lord!"

"Praise the Lord!" I exclaimed in agreement.

Pills, potty and pad . . . she was all set, and so was I. Mom back to bed; me off to work. Both of us smiling. Praise the Lord, indeed.

Tuesday, February 7, 2012

Where are her hearing aids? Oh my gosh! I forgot to take them from her last night and put them away. After I prepared eggs for breakfast and we ate, I turned her room upside down and inside out looking for the objects of my hide and seek. Nowhere to be found. I donned my rubber gloves and sorted through the bedroom and bathroom trash cans thinking the hearing aids may have been carefully wrapped in a tissue for safe keeping. Not a pleasant task by any means! Well, they were not in the trash. Where were those elusive hearing aids? I couldn't spend the day yelling much less having the TV loud enough for her to hear and to drown out the barking of the dog next door! So I searched drawers, closets, pockets, shoes—you name it—under the bed and between the sheets and blankets. Lo and behold, after stripping her bed and changing the sheets and pillowcases, there they were—a sight for sore eyes! The prodigal hearing aids were *in* a pillowcase. A thank-you-Jesus moment.

With her hearing restored, I announced to Mom, "You have to take a shower." Shedding her clothes in her bedroom, she streaked across the hall and entered her torture chamber. Have I mentioned she loathed taking a shower?

"You'll survive," I told her.

"I'm not so sure. There's always that last time. If you find me dead, you'll know what happened!"

"At least you'll be clean!" I said, laughing.

We proceeded with the cleansing. When I informed her she must wash her hair, she said, "Well, shit!" Yes, my saintly mother, who had never used inappropriate language in her life, uttered the very word about which her mother once said, "What you had in your mouth, I wouldn't hold in my hand!"

I replied, "That's pretty much how I feel about it."

Wednesday, March 14, 2012

There was more to this story, but one day last week her pad had been removed, her jeans soaked, but her bed was not wet. Depends and its gel insides were all over the bathroom floor. I cleaned it all up before leaving for school.

April 10, 2012

As I was putting Mom to bed, she was saying random syllables, almost as if she were reading a list of prefixes and suffixes. Suddenly she stopped talking and looked directly at me. "I'm not drunk, I'm just nuts!"

Laughter ensued from both of us.

April 11, 2012

Up and dressed for work, I emerged from my bedroom. Greeting me in my doorway was a faux ficus tree. This same ficus tree usually resided in a corner in Mom's room. Now the woman could barely get around, but somehow she dragged that ficus tree from her room across the hall to my doorway. Her bedroom door was open, and she was not in bed. I spied her down the hall standing in the living room and leaning on the back of the sofa. I walked over to her and asked, "What are you doing?"

"I'm too tired to go." I wasn't sure where she was planning to go, but reminded her she was retired and didn't have to go anywhere. She could go back to bed and sleep until she was rested. So we got her little routine of pills, potty, and pad completed, and she went back to bed.

I texted Philip the pictures of where I found the ficus tree, and where it was supposed to be.

"It looks better there!" he said. "But I wonder what she was thinking."

"I don't know, but she was too tired to go."

"Yes, well, landscaping is hard work!"

Where the tree greeted me.

Corner in her room where the tree used to be.

April 14, 2012

Again, the middle of the night. I found Mom on the living room sofa with pillows piled on and around her. She was sleeping soundly, so I left her in peace.

Saturday, November 24, 2012

Upon emerging from my room, I found Mom sitting on the couch in the living room. I brought us both a cup of coffee, and we chatted for a while. After we finished our first cup of coffee, we moseyed over to the table to have breakfast. Oh my gosh! Two large wet spots were on the sofa where she had been sitting. Oh no! I just stared in shock. The Depends were full and overflowing. Bring out the Febreze! Get the clothes steamer! Put the cushion in the sun! Whew!

We proceeded with her shower first and then breakfast. She was becoming physically slower and mentally unable to understand instructions and the meanings of words. Processing words, much less sentences, was becoming more challenging for her and more frustrating for me.

Friday, November 30, 2012

Got up early to go to work, and as always, got completely ready before going to check on Mom. Woke her up to go to the bathroom and take her pills. She looked at me and asked, "Where am I?"

"My house," I replied.

"When did I get here?"

"You live here. You've been here for over four years."

"Who are you?"

"I'm your daughter, Debbie."

"You are? Debbie, Debbie, Debbie, Debbie, Debbie. I'll try to remember that," she said.

I got her up, changed her underwear, took off her pajamas, put on her pants and shirt, put her back in bed, and left for work, tears trickling down my face.

Saturday, Dec. 1, 2012

Heard Mom roaming around, opening and closing doors and turning on lights at 6:00 A.M. I prayed she would find her way back to bed and go back to sleep. Praise God, she did. I went back to much needed sleep, too. Later when I got up, I found Mom sitting in the living room looking at a magazine. I greeted her and hugged her and asked if she wanted some coffee.

"Yes."

"Do you want some breakfast?"

"We haven't had breakfast yet?"

"Nope, not yet."

I brought her coffee and her hearing aids. "Let's give you the gift of hearing." I put them in her ears.

"OK. It's coming to me!" she announced.

We moved to the kitchen table for breakfast. Poured her another cup of coffee.

She said, "You are a worker."

I responded, "Yes, I am just a worker bee, and you are the queen bee!"

Mom quipped, "That's right!"

We laughed.

A couple of minutes later I set a bowl of oatmeal and a plate of toast in front of her. She asked, "What's that?"

"Oatmeal." Now I had made oatmeal for her three or four days a week for the past few years. "Do you want some banana in your oatmeal?"

"What's that?" she asked. Here we go again . . .

She continued, "I did hair when I worked. What did you do?"

"I was a teacher."

"Oh, that's good."

As I did sometimes, I sang a few notes of "Oh, what a beautiful morning. Oh, what a beautiful day!"

Mom put her hand on her chest, made a noise of some kind, and said, "Mine's broken."

We both laughed.

December 5, 2012

Mom got up really early, came to my bedroom door and wiggled the doorknob, then began opening and closing the hall doors. I whispered my familiar prayer, "Please let her find her way back to bed."

I was able to go into work a little later this morning, so I slept in before getting ready for work. By this time Mom was back in bed. I woke her up to take her pills. She was wet, her pajamas were wet, as were the sheets. A day's work before work.

Thursday, January 3, 2013

Sixty! Yes, I arrived at sixty today. I didn't much like the sound or meaning of that number. I went to bed last night about 11:45 P.M. By 12:30 A.M. Mom was bursting into my room asking, "Who are you?" and "Where should I be?" I put her back to bed. I remembered to lock my door this time.

At 1:30 A.M. she was back wiggling the doorknob on my bedroom door. Oh my gosh! I got up again to put her back to bed. She was angry because she thought she couldn't get back into the house. She was mad and raising her voice about him leaving her here. She would not settle down. In great frustration I raised my voice to her. I heard my tone and my words, but I couldn't stop myself. "Mom, go back to bed!"

"Well, he just left me here, and I don't know where I am!"

I cupped her face in my hands. "Nobody left you here. You live here. Now please go back to bed!"

"I'm just gonna shoot myself."

"Please don't shoot yourself. I'll just have to clean it up! I am your daughter, and you live here with me. I'm trying to take care of you and give you a nice place to live. It is 1:30 in the morning! The middle of the night! Please, please just get back in bed and go to sleep. I am so tired, and I've got to get some sleep!"

Back in her room and in bed, she laid down on her side and apologized. "I'm sorry. I'm sorry. I'm sorry."

"I'm sorry I raised my voice to you," I said. "I'm just tired and need some sleep."

I turned off her light, closed her bedroom door, walked the four steps back to my room, got in my bed and cried myself to sleep. I felt *horrible*! How could I yell at my mother like that? She was the dearest and sweetest little woman on the planet, and I loved her so very much. I felt so guilty. I repented to my Lord Jesus. *Please, forgive me.*

Again at 6:00 A.M., she was up and at 'em. This time, somehow, I kept my cool and gently guided her back to bed. I finally fell back to sleep until 10:25 A.M.

After my quiet time with the Lord, I emerged from my bedroom and sauntered toward the kitchen. Mom was up and sitting at the kitchen table having coffee, just as pleasant and cheerful as she could be. I prepared oatmeal for her breakfast, and she ate some of it, but was full after having consumed almost an entire pot of coffee and what appeared to be bread in her cup of coffee.

After breakfast she joined me on the sofa. I was reading my birthday cards from my friends, and I invited her to read them with me. Cheerfully she looked at them and pretended to read them. I told her it was my birthday.

"Oh, I didn't know."

"It's okay. You don't even know *who* I am."

We both had a good laugh.

I got her dressed for the day and prepared her lunch.

What a delightful surprise to find that Tom Selleck, the celebrity love of my life, was a guest on *The Talk* on CBS. A birthday miracle! A thank-you-Jesus moment.

I was out the door for a little while. Just a small break.

Sunday, February 10, 2013

Oh my gosh! Two days straight of the same questions over and over and over and *over*! Not an exaggeration. My patience was drained, completely depleted. I had none left. I could not take anymore—not just the repeating of the questions, but the behavior that went with it.

She followed me around. I could not get up and go into another room without her trying to go with me. She could not find her way to the bathroom. I had to give her directions or show her *every single time she went*! How did she make it when I was not home? She probably wandered around until she found whatever she was looking for. She couldn't just reach into the bag for some chips—she had to rattle the bag for minutes on end. Anything that came in a wrapper she struggled with until she got what she wanted. It grated on my nerves and drove me crazy.

She couldn't see, couldn't hear, couldn't process words, couldn't think of or verbalize any words. There was no coherency in her words; they sounded like babble. She was becoming physically slower and slower. Pretty soon she would be going backwards!

I had no idea why God allowed Mom to suffer this way, because she *was* suffering. I had no idea what I was supposed to learn from this experience. I just hoped I learned all I was supposed to, because I didn't want God to have to reteach me.

Mom couldn't really do anything. If I was up doing something, then every three minutes all I heard was "Need some help?" Toward the end of the day, my answers became curt and short, and I felt so guilty for answering in that kind of voice. When I put her to bed and kissed her goodnight, she thanked me, as always, for taking care of her. I said, "You're welcome," but felt like a heel.

I felt like anybody could have done a better job of being kind to her than I did today. I felt awful. Weeping uncontrollably didn't help, but it was the only thing I could do at this point. Sometimes I just walked around the house sobbing, the only coping mechanism I had at the moment. I was at the end of my rope and almost left the house just to drive around to get a break.

March 16, 2013

She told me I should have seen that little boy who kept running across the room. "I guess he's getting some exercise. Here he goes again." She laughed. Of course, there was no little boy.

March 19, 2013

Mom emerged from the hall and entered the living room. "Are you the one I'm looking for?" she asked.

"I don't know," I said. "Do you know me?"

"Well, yeah."

"Who am I?"

"A good friend? Brother? Sister?"

"I'm your daughter."

"You're the best one!"

I smiled. "I'm the best one!"

She smiled back. "You're the best one!"

Saturday, April 6, 2013

At 5:30 A.M. there was a banging sound on my bedroom door. Mom wanted to come into my room. I got up and escorted her back to her bed. At 8:00 A.M. there was more banging.

"What?" I called.

"Can I come in?" Mom asked through the door.

"Why?"

"I don't know where to go."

I invited her to come with me to the kitchen for coffee. But, on the way, we stopped by her room for her warm robe and house shoes. As I helped her put on her shoes, we talked about being tired and not getting much sleep. I mentioned that I got up at 5:30 A.M. every day to go to work, and I would like to sleep in a little on Saturday mornings.

Mom responded, "Well, everybody needs a kid to get them up."

I retorted, "Well, I have an eighty-three-year-old kid who gets me up and going."

We laughed.

"Is there a place I can get some liquid or water?" Mom asked.

We went to the kitchen, and she rinsed her hands. I gave her the meds. "Where do I go now?" she asked.

I showed her the chair at the table. She sat down, and I began to prepare oatmeal and toast for her breakfast.

"I'm sorry. I feel sorry for kids who don't have parents to take care of them."

I served the oatmeal and toast to her.

"Thanks for being so nice," Mom said, watching me.

I didn't feel very nice. A few tears escaped my eyes.

Tuesday/Wednesday April 23-24, 2013

When I returned home from work on Tuesday, all seemed well. However, looks can be deceiving. On the bathroom floor, I discovered an extremely soiled Depends. Oh my word! The toilet was filled with excrement. Overwhelming aroma. Thank God for disinfectant wipes. With so much experience, I started to clean the bathroom at warp speed! Too bad this was not an Olympic sport!

Just shy of 10:00 P.M., I tucked Mom in bed. As always, I stayed up to finish my daily chores. About 10:30 P.M. I went to bed. At 11:34 P.M. I heard glass crashing! Oh my word! Springing from my warm comfortable bed, I found Mom in the dark living room by the television. She had knocked over a glass vase of lighted flowers and a small vase of blue beads. Miracle upon miracle nothing was broken. Mom was upset; I was upset. Why was she in there? What was she doing? Who knows? She sure didn't. I righted the vases and their contents.

At 4:47 A.M. Mom was up again, therefore, so was I. Well, why not? I had to get up in 45 minutes anyway! I escorted her back to bed.

May 6, 2013

This morning, I found Mom's Depends hanging in the hall on the doorknob of her room, never a good sign. I deposited the heavy Depends in the garage trash can, then I took a deep breath and entered her room. She was asleep under the covers. I woke her, which was no easy task. She was wearing a plaid jacket over her pajama top and no pajama bottoms. The missing bottoms were draped at the head of her bed. The second she got out of bed, the urine flowed down her legs, onto the carpet, the bed, and everything in its path. *Clean up on aisle three!* And you know the rest of the story.

Wednesday, July 10, 2013

As she sat in a big overstuffed living room chair looking to her right, Mom talked in the friendliest voice to the arm of the chair. Mom was doing all of the talking, so I grabbed a pencil and paper and wrote down what she said. The conversation went like this:

"Your friend is here. Maybe she will let us go home. Anything we really need. You can rest. I'd like for you to come see me sometime and spend the week. Could you do that? No telling what we could do. That would be fun." She smiled sweetly. "I'd like for you to. Are you ready to go to bed soon?"

Saturday, July 13, 2013

It's 5:27 A.M. and oh my gosh . . . what is that crash? Did she fall, knock something over, knock some decor off of the wall? Oh my gosh . . . what *is* that banging? What is she saying?

Pushing my sleep mask onto my forehead, then arising from my cozy bed, I stumbled into the hall to check on the commotion. Her door was open, the room dark, and she was standing between the window and the chest of drawers, pounding on the wall.

"Mom, what are you doing?"

"Trying to get into the house!"

"You are *in* the house," I said.

"Well, he told me . . ."

"He is wrong. Let's go back to bed. Do you need to go to the bathroom?

"Potty?"

"Yes."

She nodded.

Mission accomplished and back to bed at 5:34 A.M.

Randomness and More Humor from Life with Mom

Discerning her left foot from her right foot was a monumental task for Mom. Hardly ever did she achieve success without some assistance. Many times she would have matching shoes on her feet, but they were on the wrong feet. Sometimes she wore her socks over her shoes. Who knew? On occasion she would have on two different shoes, one on the correct foot, but the other shoe matched neither the correct foot nor the other shoe.

One day as she was coming from the living room chair to the dinner table to eat, I noticed she could barely walk. She was just limping along. Oh my gosh! What was wrong? I reached out for her arm and helped her to the nearest chair. Was it a stroke? Did something break? She didn't appear to be in pain; she just couldn't walk.

While checking her condition, you know, doing the stroke test, I looked down at her feet, and lo and behold, she had on three shoes! Oh my word!

On her left foot, she had on a single house shoe. However, on her right foot, she had on her house shoe and a casual shoe on top of that. No wonder she had such trouble walking! We shared an exceptionally good laugh.

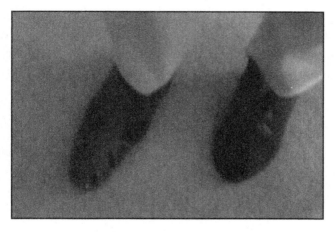

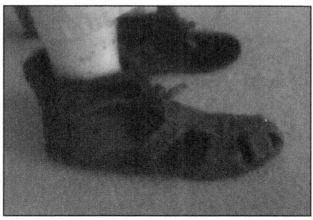

What has two feet but wears three shoes?
My little mama.

When I installed her hearing aids, I would say, "Mom, let's give you the gift of hearing." I think the aids helped me as much as they helped her.

One night after I had tucked her in, I removed her hearing aids from her ears. She said, "Well, I guess I'm going into the silent area!" Once again unexpected laughter ensued.

Sometimes she took napkins from the holder on the table into the bathroom for toilet tissue.

Rarely did she ever put the used tissue into the toilet or even the trash. Instead she would deposit it onto the floor or in the tub or in the sink. I should have bought stock in drain cleaners and disinfectant wipes.

Many times instead of pouring coffee into a coffee cup, she would pour the coffee into the sugar bowl. Hence, I didn't keep more than a couple of teaspoons of sugar in the bowl, and eventually I hid the bowl altogether.

Regarding indoor bathrooms, Mom would say, "When I get home, I'm going to get me one of those." Good idea, Mom.

Whenever we sat down to eat, she never remembered where she sat. Never! Even after years of me patting the chair seat and saying "This is your chair, Mom. You always sit right here."

Sometimes when I was just a little late coming home from work, I would find her packing her clothes or would find her clothes and various things already packed in plastic grocery bags. She was getting ready to go home. So, I would "talk her down" and unpack her bags and put everything back in her closet and chest of drawers.

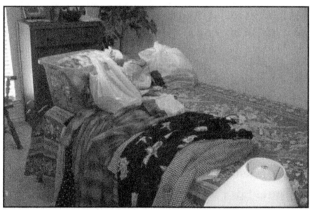

When my friends would call and talk for any length of time, Mom somehow thought I needed privacy, so she retreated to her room and began taking things out of the chest of drawers and closet and placing them on her bed. Later "we" had to put everything away before she could go to bed.

A couple of times when I returned home from work or from doing errands, I found her sitting by the phone trying to call her mother to come and take her home. She was homesick for a home that no longer existed.

The conversations she initiated were many times quite bizarre. They always began with questions. Here are some samplings.

Mom: "Have I been bad the last few days?"

Me: "Mom, you are never bad. You are always good."

Mom: "I might do things I don't know. But I don't mean to. I have a bad feeling for you people."

Mom: "Do you know where my husband is? Have you seen him this afternoon?"

Me: "Your husband is my father."

Mom, opening her eyes as wide and surprised as I had ever seen them: "He is? Are you my mother?"

Me: "I am your daughter. Your husband, my father, passed away several years ago."

Mom: "Do you know if I live with my daughter? Does she work? Is she in school, or is she working? She's sixteen isn't she? You may be the one."

Me: "I am the one."

Mom: "I'm glad you told me about that."

Mom: "Where are we? Whose house is this?"

Me: "We are in my house."

Mom: "Do I get money?"

Me: "Yes, you get a Social Security check."

Mom: "I am thankful for you. Proud that you're my daughter. You're an angel. Will we stay here tonight? I guess I could drive my car down to my house. You think?"

Me: "No, I don't think so, Mom."

Mom: "I don't know if there's anybody else down at my house."

At 6:30 P.M. one evening, she used the walker to go down the hall and back. She wanted to know if "we needed to tie that down."

I was thinking, *tie what down*?

"It might save us some money."

I still had no idea what she meant.

She abandoned the walker and furniture-surfed over to the sofa to sit down and watch *Wheel of Fortune*.

At 6:44 P.M. she turned and said, "Don't forget me when you leave."

"I'm not leaving."

"Oh, you're not? I'll stay with you."

Mom: "Do you have a name?"

Me: "Yes."

Mom: "What is it?"

Me: "Debbie. You gave it to me."

Mom: "Oh."

Me: "You are my mother. I am your daughter."

One day Mom was sitting on the sofa smiling and making baby faces. She said, "When I leave here this afternoon, remind me to bring this baby with me."

Baby? What baby?

"This baby sure is still," Mom said.

That's because it's a sofa pillow, Mom!

She gently touched the pillow and said, "I'm not sure it's alive. Her eyes don't move." She moved her face closer to the pillow.

"Mom," I said, "it's a pillow."

"Oh, so she won't get too cold then." She moved the pillow closer to her and said, "I need to get this baby to Philip."

Early on I would take Mom to the grocery store with me. She would push the grocery cart because it gave her some exercise, and the cart helped to steady her. Sometimes she would bump the cart into things or shelves. When that happened, I would tell her, "Mama, that's why we don't let you drive." . . . Well, I thought it was funny.

Even though she couldn't move very well in the daytime, at night Mom seemed to acquire superhuman strength. Like when she moved the faux ficus from her room to the bathroom. She also once stuffed the top of the tree between the toilet and the tub, leaving the bottom lying at the other end of the tub. Go figure.

June 11, 2013

I met my cousin for lunch and then did a few errands on the way home. As usual I drove down my alley and pushed the garage door opener. *Uh-oh.* The door from the garage to the house was open, and that was never a good sign. As was my routine, I put the car in reverse and backed into the garage. About halfway in, I hit a bump and heard a squeal. I pulled forward, put the car in park, and got out of the car to see what was going on.

I spied her feet and legs. Mom was lying on the garage floor!

I screamed, "Mom, are you okay? What happened? Did I knock you down? Did you fall?"

Her eyes were open. She was alive, but she didn't know how she got there. Her pants were down around her knees . . . one shoe was off. She was lying on her left side facing the inside garage wall.

I yelled, "I'm calling 911!"

She yelled back, "No! No! No! No! NO!"

In the sternest of voices, I said, "Then you better get up!"

I checked for pain, broken bones, bleeding. No pain, no blood, no apparent broken bones. And she seemed surprisingly coherent.

I pulled her pants up and moved her to a sitting position. I looked around the garage thinking about how I was going to get her in the house. Aha! The wheelchair! I moved it closer and locked the wheels. Taking advantage of my adrenalin rush, I put my arms under her armpits, picked her up, and put her in the wheelchair. I rolled her into the house and commanded her to "stay put!"

Assured that she was okay, I quickly brought in the bag of groceries. Then I spied a very round piece of fecal matter on the floor in the utility room. How it morphed into that shape I had no idea; none whatsoever. But, thank God for plastic trash bags and disinfectant wipes! After inspecting Mom's clothes, I discovered a tire mark on the back of her sweatshirt near the top, and feces on her underwear and on the hem of her pants.

The shower was her next activity. I found two huge scrapes on her left hip and upper thigh, and her left elbow was bruised and skinned. Praise God she had no pain or broken bones. While she was in the shower, on the other side of the curtain, I leaned against the bathroom wall and with my head in my hands, I quietly sobbed. I could have killed my mother! What if I hadn't heard the squeal? What if I hadn't gotten out to check? A million "what ifs" went through my mind.

Enough! Stop it!

I got her dressed, and she rested in a big comfy chair.

Now the questions remained: Why was my mother in the garage, lying on the floor. Even more puzzling, why were her pants down below her knees?

Being a huge fan of *NCIS* and similar shows using logic and deductive reasoning, I decided to look at the evidence.

Evidence:

- Two overturned plastic trash cans—one small round one; one tall rectangular one
- The tall rectangular one was split and broken at the top of one of its short sides
- Paper dinner napkins from the holder on the kitchen table were strewn about near the broken trash can

- Mom's pants were down around her knees
- One shoe off
- Feces in the utility room on the way to the garage
- Urine in the trash can.

I deduced she took napkins to use as toilet paper, went into the garage and used the rectangular trash can as the toilet. When it broke from her weight as she sat down, she fell to the floor. The shoe off and the orb-shaped feces were still a puzzle.

Friday, July 26, 2013

Today was the big day. My stomach was in knots. Mom and I ate breakfast together. I knew it was our last breakfast together at home, but did she? Apparently the conversations we had been having for a few months had found a place to reside in her brain, because as we were eating she said about herself, "She is not going to be here much longer is she?"

Replying in the most cheerful and reassuring voice I could muster, I said, "No, you are going to a great new place today. You won't have to stay by yourself anymore during the day, and nurses will be with you to help when you need anything. You will have your own room and your own bed, and they bring your meals to you. Doesn't that sound good?"

"Yes, it does. Will you be there?"

"No, I have to work. But I will come see you often, and you will make lots of new friends. It will be just like living in a college dorm." She never lived in a college dorm but visited me in mine. Whew!

After her shower, we got her dressed, and off we went to her hair appointment at 11:00 A.M. at the care facility. While she was getting her hair done, I prepared her room. After her hair appointment, my plan was to take her to the dining room for lunch. I would leave while she was eating and chatting with the other residents. I had saturated this event in prayer, so I knew God would be faithful. After her hair was done, I said, "Let's go see your new room." We then went to the dining room, and I sat her at a table with some other ladies. While she was having lunch, I finished up with the office personnel.

After lunch there were several visitors in the visitation area/dining hall, and I managed to seat Mom among them. While everyone was visiting, I managed to leave unnoticed by Mom. I walked through the secured doors and down the hall and out to my car.

Oh my goodness! Sitting in my car for a few minutes, I took some time to gather myself and take several deep breaths. God was so very faithful. Since I had something to do and someplace to be, I started the car and left. I had promised to help set up for my great-niece's second birthday party. It was strange not to have to be home before dark, and not to have to worry about what I would find when I arrived home.

An eerie, but welcomed silence greeted me when I arrived home later that evening. It felt very, very weird. A myriad of emotions swept over me all at the same time—relief, sadness, guilt, exhaustion . . . just to name a few. It was late, so I went to bed.

Saturday, July 27, 2013

I was up early to go to my great-niece's birthday party. Great fun. Again, no time restraints. Wow, no curfew!

Because I was wisely advised not to return to the care facility for at least the weekend, I decided on Sunday I would thoroughly clean Mom's room and bathroom. Since she was having some dental work and oral surgery done soon, and I wanted to avoid the temptation of bringing her back to my house to recuperate, I thoroughly cleaned, washed, and scrubbed her room and bathroom. It took me all day and was very therapeutic. I just let the emotions flow as I worked. Purging emotions with physical cleaning seemed to work for me. I knew it wouldn't be the last time I needed to express or release pent-up feelings, but it was a very good start.

Second Corinthians 1:3-4 states, "Blessed be the God and Father of our Lord Jesus Christ, the Father of mercies and God of all comfort, who comforts us in all our affliction, so that we may be able to comfort those who are in any affliction, with the comfort with which we ourselves are comforted by God."

I have to believe the experiences during this journey Mom and I took, and are continuing to take, are not in vain. Hopefully you have received from this book something to meet a need of yours and bring you comfort and validation of your own emotions. Without a doubt, God blessed Mom and me throughout our journey.

Hopefully, my purposes for writing this book have been achieved. My hope is that the millions of unpaid caregivers will recognize their experiences are universal, shared, and at the same time, personal and unique to them.

I hope you have begun thinking about provisions for your own elder care or the care of someone you love. If you know caregivers, please give them support and encouragement. Listen to them and be patient. Please don't offer advice unless they ask for it.

Since Mom moved into the long-term care facility, our visits have become sweeter and less stressful, at least for me. Not having to provide for her physical needs lifted a burden from me. I can see her any time I want, so I visit her about four times each week, and I still do her laundry. Because there is probably a short window of time left in which she can interact with me, I have begun to really look forward to seeing her and loving on her. Holding her hands and kissing her on the cheek or forehead are more precious to me every time I visit her. I do miss her.

When I get ready to leave, I always kiss her on the forehead and/or cheek and say, "I love you, Mama."

She responds, "I love you, too." Once she said, "I love you always."

Even though she doesn't know *who* I am, she recognizes me as "the one who takes care of her," or that I'm "important," or I'm "the main one."

On a Sunday several months after she moved into the long-term care facility, I brought lunch to her. I took her out to the main lobby where we shared Sunday dinner, as we have done many, many times in our lives.

While I was feeding her ice cream, she said, "Do you work here?"

I said, "No, I just came to see you."

She smiled so big and said, "Wonderful. Thank you."

I smiled back. Sometimes after I visit with her I leave laughing, and sometimes I leave crying.

My very sweet Mother Keys

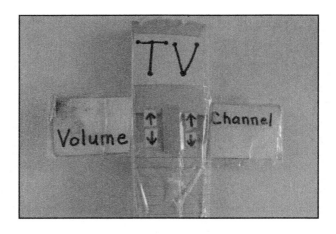

Tips and Tactics

In the mornings when I left for work, I left the television turned on. To make TV watching less confusing for her, I covered all of the buttons on the TV remote using green index cards and yellow paper secured by clear tape. I labeled only the channel selection and volume control with black magic marker. I cleared the coffee table of everything but the remote so it would be easy for her to find. This worked for a while, especially in the beginning.

Along our arduous journey, I tried to schedule breaks for myself, often just a few hours and sometimes a few days. If you are a caregiver, I highly recommend you take as many breaks as you think you need. Don't wait until you are too stressed out to enjoy the respite.

So my substitute caregiver would be at ease, I prepared a pertinent and comprehensive three-ring notebook of information addressing everything from medications to bedtime routine. If I was out for an evening, I always left dinner prepared for Mom and her caregiver. If I was gone for a couple of days, I left food to reheat or easy to prepare so he or she would come back!

In order to take full advantage of my respite, I did not call or text to check on things. I let the caregiver call or text me if a problem arose. No news was good news in this case.

When she first moved in with me, Mom was able to manage some things on her own while I was at work. So, in the mornings I left her medication cup with her pills and her cups with her hearing aids in them on the kitchen table. I would call her mid-morning to make sure she had taken her medicine and put in her hearing aids. So she and I would not get her hearing aids mixed up, I created a storage contraption, clearly labeling each one to avoid confusion. That worked for a while in the beginning. Letting her monitor her medication was the first aspect of her life she had to relinquish. At first, using the labeled cups (in the pictures) worked well. However, as her disease progressed, I had to assume that responsibility for her.

Knowing she had to eat during the day, I came up with a solution that seemed to be successful, at least for Mom. On the kitchen table at her usual place, I would leave:

- a certain amount of cereal (some form of Cheerios) in an easy-open container
- a banana or two
- a small amount of peanut butter in a jar
- Three or four slices of bread in a bag
- a plastic plate, a spoon, and a table knife.

It was easier to manage if I measured out the amounts rather than leave the whole jar of peanut butter, the entire loaf of bread, or the whole box of cereal. I refilled each container as needed. Less mess to clean up when I got home, and she would not be too full to eat a good dinner.

For some reason Mom liked to keep her cane here in this position. She thought it was out of everyone's way. She didn't want to bother anyone.

Thank God for flip locks on the exit doors.
They saved me on many nights.

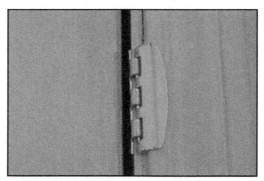

Flip lock open so that the door opens freely

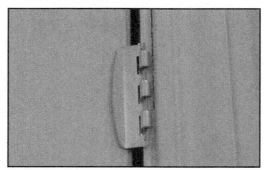

Flip lock closed at the top or bottom of the door frame

- I always dressed and was ready for the day before I checked on her in the mornings.
- I labeled the drawers of the dresser/chest in her room. It helped me when putting away her clothes, and it was also helpful for others who stayed with her when I was out.
- Staying involved with family and friends is absolutely essential. Do not let yourself or your loved one become isolated. When Mom was able, I took her with me when my friends and I went out for a casual dinner. When she became less mobile, I invited my friends over for dinner. I prepared the main dish, and they brought food to share.
- Take your own advice.
- Ask for help.
- Let the sitters call you. You shouldn't call while you are on a break.
- Lock your bedroom door during the day while you are gone and at night to avoid any unexpected or unwanted intrusions.
- Keep a current working list of needs. When someone offers to help—you know the offer— "Let me know if there is anything I can do to help"—refer to your list. Select something like staying with your loved one while you go shopping, or to the grocery store, or go see a movie, or go to the park, or whatever you need to get out and do. I have found that people are more than willing to help; they just need guidance.

- Invite your family and friends over to visit for a little while. It gives you someone to talk to and helps them become more familiar with your loved one's condition and your routine in case you need a sitter.
- Maintain a three-ring binder of instructions and any pertinent information for anyone who stays with your loved one. *Include a list of current medications, insurance information and information regarding allergies to take to the hospital in case of an emergency.*
- Keep a journal or at least a calendar. It provides a form of stress relief, improves your memory, helps adjust your perspective, keeps you honest, and provides concrete evidence to recognize when you need a break or respite.
- Using plastic sheet protectors and binder clips, I changed the info on this display every day, hoping Mom could read it and be assured I would be home later in the day. I wanted her to feel as secure as possible. I set up the display on the fireplace hearth near the TV so she would be sure to see it.

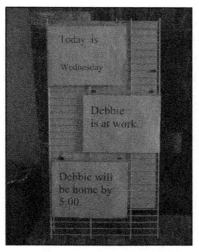

- On a large piece of paper, I taped my cell phone number to my home phone in case she needed to call me.
- Unless it is an emergency, wait twenty-four hours before approving any change in medication or treatment. Take that time to do your research; then follow your gut.
- Take a list of questions and concerns to all doctor appointments. Take notes during the visit. Don't rely on your memory.
- Most importantly, if you are a caregiver for a loved one who resides in a care facility, *do not* leave any care meeting without a copy of everything discussed, prescribed, and signed by you or anyone. Take a few minutes to read

what you are signing. Ask them nicely to make copies on the spot while you wait. Taking notes during all meetings proved to be valuable to me in being an advocate for my mother.

Sign I taped to the inside of the front door
to stop her from wandering outside.

Author's Note

*J*n July of 2013, I entered a caregiver "Rest and Recharge" contest sponsored by A Place for Mom. My essay won, and I was awarded a three-day respite at Joan Lunden's Camp Reveille in Maine. It was awesome! This is the picture of Mom and me that accompanied the article in the *Dallas Morning News,* "Neighborsgo" section, announcing my good fortune.

Why Do You Think I Call You Mama?

In May of 2015, I entered a Mother's Day essay contest sponsored by A Place for Mom, and I was selected as one of the winners. My mother's beloved pastor read my essay at her funeral, and I share it with you now:

A PTM Mother's Day Essay

*T*o say my mom means the world to me is an understatement. Without "preaching", she modeled the finest qualities a woman could possess. She taught me faith in God, compassion, independence, confidence, integrity, perseverance, and unconditional love.

During our Sunday family dinners after church, we would all share stories of the week while enjoying Mom's home cooking. She exemplified a true Southern lady because, not only was the food delicious, but there was always more than enough to feed everyone.

Another cherished memory of my childhood was getting off of the school bus, racing into the house for an after-school snack and discovering a new handmade dress for my Barbie doll. I still treasure a pink one trimmed with rickrack. What a precious memory to me.

For more years than she would want me to reveal, she was a beautician, and her beauty shop was connected to our house. When we got home from elementary school, Mom would let my brother and me go into the beauty shop, and while she worked, we would tell her about our day at school. We loved it, and honestly, her customers didn't seem to mind. I think we were free entertainment!

In her mid-teens, she won a beauty contest, but a head-on car crash in early 1959 left her with many scars from many surgeries. However, in my mind, these scars did not mar her physical or inner beauty. A scar from her bottom right chin diagonally up across her mouth to the bottom left corner of her nose made her smile that much more endearing. A crushed and ultimately missing kneecap altered her gait a bit, but she remained a very active mom and grandmother.

After she was diagnosed with dementia, she moved in with me. At night I would tuck her into bed. One night in particular, as I was tucking her in, she started babbling, saying nonsensical syllables. She stopped abruptly, looked at me directly in the eyes, and my sweet-tea-drinking little Southern Baptist mother exclaimed, "I'm not drunk. I'm just nuts!" We both burst into laughter that filled every corner of the room.

On one of my recent visits to the nursing home where she resides, she summed up our relationship so succinctly when I said to her, "I love you Mama," and she responded with "I love you all the time."

With her children by her side, my sweet mom went to be with her Lord on June 3, 2015.

CPSIA information can be obtained at www.ICGtesting.com
Printed in the USA
BVOW06*0354260216

438115BV00003B/3/P